Footprints of Love:
- Verses on Life and Beyond

Reema Wadhwa

BookLeaf Publishing

India | USA | UK

Footprints of Love: - Verses on Life and Beyond © 2024 Reema Wadhwa

All rights reserved.

No part of this publication may be reproduced, stored in a retrieval system, or transmitted, in any form or by any means, electronic, mechanical, photocopying, recording or otherwise, without the prior written permission of the presenters.

Reema Wadhwa asserts the moral right to be identified as the author of this work.

Presentation by *BookLeaf Publishing*

Web: www.bookleafpub.com

E-mail: info@bookleafpub.com

ISBN:9789360947620

First edition 2024

DEDICATION

I dedicate this book, 'Footprints of Life: Verses on Life and Beyond,' to my father, who I know is watching over me from heaven. Papa, I hope this work makes you proud, just as you always inspired me to be my best.

To my mother, your unwavering love and support have been my rock. This book is as much yours as it is mine, for without you, none of this would be possible.

To my husband and friends, thank you for being my pillars of strength and sources of inspiration. Your belief in me has been a driving force behind this endeavor.

I am grateful to all those who have touched my life in ways big and small, thank you for being a part of my journey. This book is as much yours as it is mine.

ACKNOWLEDGEMENT

In the quiet spaces between words, where stories unfold and dreams take flight, there lie the echoes of those who have touched my life and this book in profound ways.

To my Father in heaven, who whispers inspiration in the wind and paints the sky with words, thank you for guiding my pen and illuminating my path.

To my mother, a beacon of unwavering support and love, your belief in me has been the light that has guided me through the darkest of nights.

To my husband, whose patience, understanding, and love have sustained me through this journey, I am endlessly grateful.

To my friends, who have listened, encouraged, and believed in me, thank you for being the pillars of strength on which I lean.

I extend my deepest gratitude to the team at BookLeaf Publishing for their professionalism, expertise, and unwavering support in bringing this book to life.

And to you, dear reader, for embarking on this journey with me, thank you for giving my words a home in your heart.

PREFACE

In a world increasingly digital, where screens dominate and keyboards click, I find solace in the simplicity of pen and paper. From the earliest days of my education, I've been drawn to the written word, its power to express the deepest of emotions and the most profound of thoughts.

However, life has a way of reshaping our priorities and shifting our perspectives. The unexpected passing of my father during the tumult of the Covid-19 pandemic was a seismic event, altering the very fabric of my existence. In the wake of this loss, I found myself grappling with profound questions about life, love, and the bonds that tie us together.

It is from this place of introspection and transformation that this book of poetry has emerged. Each verse, each line, is a reflection of the new lens through which I now view the world. Themes of love, loss, and the enduring nature of relationships permeate these pages, echoing the timeless bond I share with my father, a bond that transcends the boundaries of life and death.

I dedicate this book to my parents, especially my father, whose blessings continue to inspire me. My mother, my pillar of strength, has been my unwavering support throughout this journey. To my husband and my dear friends, thank you for being my guiding light in the darkness.

As you turn the pages of this book, I invite you to join me on a journey of reflection, introspection, and ultimately, celebration. For in these words, I hope you find echoes of your own experiences, reminders of the beauty and complexity of the human condition.

With heartfelt gratitude,
Reema

Eternal Love

In the vast expanse of time and space,
There is a bond that nothing can erase.
It's a love that's eternal and true,
A bond between me and you.

From the moment I was born,
This bond was already sworn.
A love that knows no end,
A bond that the universe did send.

Through the years, through the tears,
Through the joys, through the fears.
This love has remained steadfast,
A bond that will forever last.

In every birth, in every life,
This bond remains, free from strife.
A piece of us in every form,
A love that's weathered every storm.

A mother-daughter bond,
Nine months older than any other,
A love so deep, a bond like no other.

So here's to you, my dear parents,
For the love that's always apparent.
For the bond that's always true,
For the love that binds me to you.

In every life, in every birth,
Our love survives, beyond the earth.
A love that's eternal and true,
A bond between me and you.

Love's Journey: A Path of Light

In the fabric of life, love weaves its thread,
A journey of the heart, where dreams are fed.
It starts with a glance, a smile, a touch so light,
A spark ignites, setting our hearts alight.

As we walk hand in hand, down love's winding
road,
We share our stories, lighten each other's load.
Through laughter and tears, we learn and grow,
Love's gentle whispers guide us as we go.

In love's embrace, we find our truest selves,
A mirror reflecting our hopes and dreams on
shelves.
We stumble and fall, but love lifts us high,
Teaching us to spread our wings and fly.

Love's journey is not always smooth or straight,
We face challenges, overcome by love's innate
Strength to endure, to forgive, to heal,
A bond so deep, nothing can conceal.

In the quiet moments, love speaks in a hush,
A language only two hearts can blush.
In every gesture, every word, every sigh,
Love's melody plays, soaring high.

Let us cherish this journey of love,
A gift from the heavens, like a gentle dove.
In its ups and downs, its twists and turns,
Love's journey teaches us, forever it yearns.

In the end, it's not the destination that we seek,
But the journey itself, the love that makes us
weak.
For in love's journey, we find our true worth,
A light that shines brightly, illuminating our
earth.

Reflection on Our Cosmic Significance

In the endless depth of the cosmos, we are but a
speck,
A tiny fragment of life, on a cosmic trek.
Millions of galaxies, stars that twinkle bright,
We are just a flicker of light, in the endless
night.

In the grand scheme of things, we are small,
A mere fraction of it all, yet we stand tall.
We are part of nature's intricate design,
A piece of the puzzle, in the grand divine.

Like dust in the wind, we float and sway,
In the dance of life, we find our way.
In the end, to dust we shall return,
A cycle of life, a lesson to learn.

Let us marvel at the universe's grandeur,
At the stars that shine, with a radiant fervor.
For in this vast cosmic play, we have a part,
A small piece of the puzzle, a work of art.

The Human Experience

In our hearts, we feel a multitude of emotions,
From the highs of happiness to the lows of
sadness.
We seek connection with others,
Yearning to be understood, to find our place in
the world.

We experience grief and sorrow, profound and
deep,
Yet through the darkness, a glimmer of hope we
keep.
Our minds are a whirlwind of thoughts,
Racing, pondering, seeking understanding.

Emotions are complex, hard to understand,
Our minds racing, like grains of sand.
But in the depths of our despair,
There's a love that's always there.

There's that one person, a guiding light,
Who's with us through every plight.
Nature and the universe, they test our will,
But with love by our side, we can climb any hill.

For in nature's love, in the love of another,
We find the strength to recover.
In every trial, in every test, Love guides us, and
we are blessed.

So let us embrace the full spectrum of our
emotions,
For in them lies the essence of our human
experience.
In our doubts, our fears, our grief, and our joy,
We find meaning, we find purpose, we find our
true selves.

Beyond Fear

In the realm of possibility, where dreams take
flight,
Where the horizon is limitless, and the future is
bright.
How big would you dream, if failure was not a
fear,
If success was certain, and obstacles
disappeared?

Would you reach for the stars, and touch the
moon,
Would you chart new paths, in the light of noon?
Would you dare to dream, of things yet unseen,
Of possibilities untold, of places unseen?

In the canvas of your mind, paint a picture bold,
Of a life well-lived, of stories yet untold.

Imagine the heights you could reach, the goals
you could attain,
If you let go of doubt, and embrace your inner
flame.

For dreams are the seeds of greatness, waiting to
be sown,
They are the fuel for your journey, the path you
must own.
So dream big, dream bold, for the world is your
stage,
And your dreams are the key to unlock your
cage.

Unseen Bond

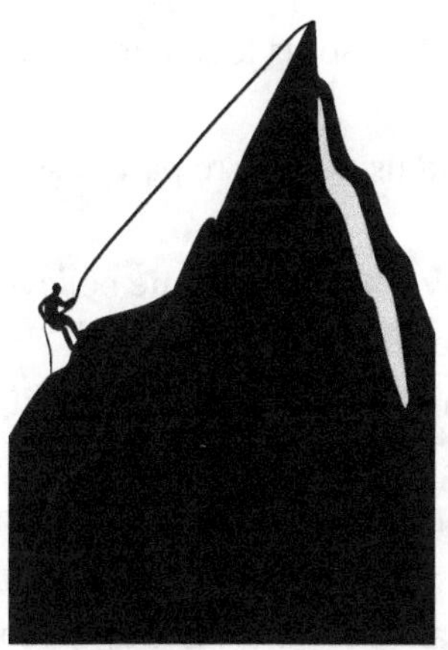

Sometimes you meet someone, and everything
aligns.
Out of nowhere, a connection so deep,
A feeling of being alive, of being in sync, a bond
to keep.

It might be a friend, a family member, or a lover,
Or it might be a stranger, like no other.
But in that moment, it doesn't matter who they
are,
What matters is the connection, like a guiding
star.

I don't know if it's coincidence or fate,
Or just the universe's way, its intricate trait.

But I believe in something, in that magical
spark,
That brings two souls together, even in the dark.

They remind us that we're part of something
grand.
I don't know if that makes me believe in
coincidence, sheer luck or fate,
But it definitely makes me believe in something.

I'll cherish these moments, these connections so
true,
For they make me believe, they give me a clue.
That there's a plan in place, a purpose in sight,
And in these connections, everything feels right.

Embrace Change

In the flow of life's river, as days turn to years,
Change is the constant, amid hopes and fears.
No matter the season, no matter the tide,
Change is the force, where destinies glide.

With each passing moment, the world
transforms,
Nothing stays the same, as life reforms.
We may resist, we may fear the unknown,
But change is the only constant ever shown.

Bravery lies in saying goodbye to the old,
In welcoming the new, in being bold.
"If nothing changes, nothing changes," they say,
So let's step into the future, let's find our own
way.

Close the door to the past, open the door to the
new chapter,
Take a deep breath, the change is overdue.
Day by day, as time slips by,
Change is inevitable, we can't deny.

Einstein said, "Insanity is doing the same thing
expecting change,"
So let's break the cycle, let's rearrange.
Reflect on the days gone by, plan for the days
ahead,
Change is the only constant, in life's thread.

For those who change, survival is assured,
For those who embrace change, success is
secured.
For those who drive change, leadership is found,
Change is the rhythm, in life's profound journey.

As we welcome each day,
Let's embrace change,
Plan for change, start the change, become better,
For change is the essence, in life's letter.

Finding Happiness Within

In the pursuit of happiness, we often look
outside,
Seeking in the world, what's within us to abide.
But true joy, elusive, is not in what we find,
It's in the depths of our soul, in the heart and
mind.

In the material world, where desires bloom and
fade,
Happiness seems fleeting, like a passing shade.
We chase after riches, fame, and worldly gain,
Only to find emptiness, sorrow, and pain.

But if we pause, and look within our core,
We'll find a treasure trove, waiting to explore.
Happiness lies in gratitude, in love and in peace,

In the simple joys of life, that never cease.

It's in the laughter of a child, the warmth of a
friend,
In the beauty of nature, that knows no end.
Happiness is not a destination, but a way of
being,
Finding joy in every moment, in every fleeting
thing.

Let's stop seeking happiness outside,
And turn our gaze inwards, where it resides.
For true happiness is not in what we possess,
But in the love, kindness, and joy we express.

Passage of Time

As time slips through our fingers like sand,
Let's cherish each moment, hand in hand.
Creating memories that will forever last,
In the story of time, preserving the past.

Let's live each day with joy and cheer,
Keeping our surroundings vibrant and clear.
Lifting each other up, in times of need,
For time is a fleeting thing, with great speed.

We must be mindful of how we spend each day,
For time marches on, never to delay.
It's the moments we create, the love we share,
That truly define us, showing how much we
care.

In the quiet of the night, as the stars softly glow,
We reflect on the moments that make our hearts grow.
The laughter, the tears, the moments so dear,
They all become memories, crystal clear.

Let's embrace each day with open hearts,
For time is a gift, where our journey starts.
Let's make each moment count, in every way,
For time is the only thing that becomes a memory the next day.

Memories

In the gallery of our minds, memories hang like
art,
Each one a masterpiece, a story from the heart.
They're the echoes of our past, whispers in the
breeze,
A gallery of moments, framed with ease.

Some memories are like diamonds, precious and
clear,
Others, like watercolors, soft and near.
Memories make us who we are, strong and bold,
They're the stories of our journey, beautifully
told.

Memories are the footprints we leave behind,
In the sands of time, where our stories unwind.

They're the echoes of voices, long since gone,
Yet their essence lingers, like a lingering song.

Some memories are like gentle caresses on the
skin,
Soft and tender, comforting us from within.
Others are like jagged rocks, sharp and unkind,
Leaving scars on our hearts, etched in our mind.

But it's through memories, we learn and grow,
They're the seeds of wisdom that we sow.
They teach us to cherish, to love, and to forgive,
To embrace life fully, for as long as we live.

So let's treasure our memories, the bitter and the
sweet,
For they're the milestones that mark our life's
fleet.
Let's hold them close, and never let them fade,
For in our memories, our true selves are laid.

Loss and Heal

Loss is the void left behind,
When something dear we cannot find.
It's the ache in the heart, the tear in the eye,
The silent scream, the unanswered "why?"

Healing is the journey we embark upon,
To mend the pieces of our hearts that are drawn.
It's the courage to face each new day,
And find a new path when the old one's astray.

The process of healing is unique to each,
Some find solace in words, others in reach.
It's a journey of ups and downs, of twists and
turns,
A path that teaches, a path that burns.

The mindset of the one who heals,

Is one of strength, of faith that appeals.
It's a belief in tomorrow, a trust in the unseen,
A knowing that life goes on, despite what has
been.

Emotions run wild, in turmoil they swirl,
Grief and anger, sadness and twirl.
But in the midst of this storm, there's a glimmer
of light,
A hope for a new dawn, a promise of flight.

It's embracing the journey, however long it may
be,
For in healing, we find ourselves, we find our
key.
To unlock the pain, to release the sorrow,
And step into a new tomorrow.

Magic of New Beginnings

In the soft embrace of a morning's kiss,
Where dewdrops glisten, a moment of bliss.
There lies magic, in the birth of a day,
A chance to begin anew, come what may.

Like a painter with a blank canvas before,
We stand at the threshold of an open door.
The universe whispers, "It's time to start,"
To trust in the journey, to follow the heart.

Feathers float gently from the cosmic world,
Guiding our steps along the way.
Angel numbers shimmer, a divine sign,
In the magic of beginnings, we find the divine.

Beginnings can be daunting, a path unknown,
But they carry seeds that are sown.
In the fertile soil of hope and belief,
Beginnings unfold, dispelling grief.

Trust the process come what may,
Magic happens when we least expect its way.
For in the day of hope we all live,
Maybe because that's the only way we aspire to relive.

Life's Uncertainty

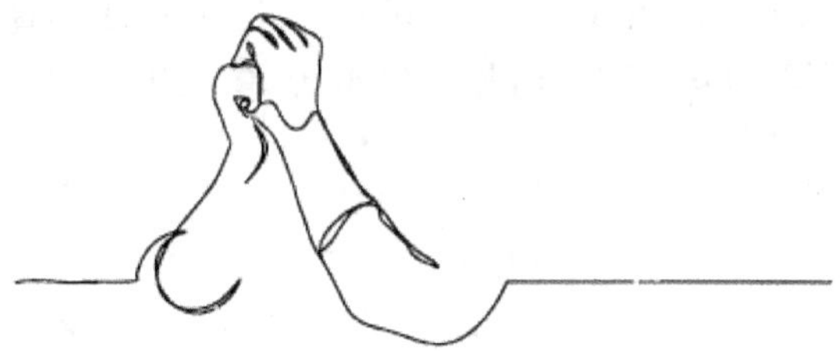

In the stillness of night, life takes a turn,
Unforeseen, unexpected, lessons to learn.
A knock at the door, a call on the line,
Changes everything, in the blink of an eye.

A virus, a threat, unseen yet so near,
Bringing the world to a standstill, in fear.
Plans put on hold, dreams shattered, it seems,
Life as we knew it, ripped at the seams.

Adaptation, resilience, the need of the hour,
To face the unknown, to gather the power.
Lessons of gratitude, for what we possess,
A reminder of life's unpredictable mess.

In the face of adversity, we find our strength,
In the depth of despair, we go to great lengths.
Life's unpredictability, a truth we must face,
With courage and hope, we embrace the race.

We stand tall, in the midst of the storm,
For in every challenge, a chance to transform.
Life's twists and turns, may catch us by surprise,
But in the depths of uncertainty, our spirits will
rise.

Acceptance and Letting Go

In the sphere of life, where moments unfold,
There lived a soul, with stories untold.
Stress was a shadow, that followed along,
Whispering worries, where once there was song.

Days turned to nights, and nights into days,
Caught in a cycle, of anxious ways.
But deep in the heart, a voice softly said,
"Let go of the worry, let go of the dread."

With each passing moment, a lesson was
learned,
That stress and its burdens, no longer he
yearned.
For in acceptance, a freedom was found,

In letting go, peace did abound.

The weight of the world, lifted off his chest,
As he embraced the present, and let go of the
rest.
No longer a prisoner, to worries and fears,
He danced with life, through laughter and tears.

So if ever you find, stress knocking at your door,
Remember this tale, and worry no more.
For in acceptance and letting go, lies the key,
To a life of peace, joyful and free.

Roots of Love

In the garden of my heart, I plant seeds of love,
Deep and true, each one a connection,
A part of me, entwined with you.

With every laugh, every tear,
Roots grow deeper, stronger, entwined,
Binding us, year after year,
In a bond that's pure and kind.

When you left, a piece of me departed too,
A void in my heart, a sky without blue.
Yet in the vast expanse of the cosmic sea,
I feel your presence, your love surrounding me.

In the whisper of the wind, in the warmth of the
sun,
In the twinkle of the stars when the day is done.

Your essence lingers, a timeless embrace,
A bond unbroken, through time and space.

Though you're not here, I feel you near,
In every moment, in every tear.
Our bond transcends the earthly plane,
A love eternal, unbound by pain.

I carry you with me, in my heart you'll stay,
A cosmic connection, guiding my way.
For even in the vastness of the universe above,
Our love remains, a testament to eternal love.

A Wish Beyond Bounds

I wish for wings to fly so high,
Above the clouds, up in the sky.
To dance with stars, to touch the moon,
In the velvet night, a magical tune.

I wish for a voice that echoes strong,
A song of peace, a world where we belong.
Where hatred fades, and love is king,
In every heart, a joyful ring.

I wish for eyes that truly see,
Beyond the surface, to what could be.
To see beauty in every soul,
To make broken hearts once again whole.

I wish for hands that heal and mend,
To reach out to others, to every friend.
To wipe away tears, to hold them tight,
To bring back hope, in the darkest night.

I wish for a mind as vast as the sea,
To dream big, to set thoughts free.
To imagine worlds, yet unseen,
To turn the ordinary into the supreme.

I wish for a heart that's brave and true,
To stand up for what's right, to see things
through.
To love fiercely, without any fear,
To make a difference, year after year.

I wish for these things, not just for me,
But for everyone, for all to see.
For wishes are more than just a dream,
They're a spark, a light, a powerful beam.

Gratitude is the Attitude of Life

In the domain of the heart, where emotions reside,
There's a place for gratitude, where blessings abide.
It's the attitude of life, the key to the divine,
A language the Universe speaks, in every design.

With Sabr and Shukr, we navigate life's course,
Patiently embracing its twists and its force.
For gratitude is more than a fleeting feeling,
It's a vibration, a frequency, in the universe's ceiling.

With each word of thanks, a ripple is sent,
A wave of positivity, through which we are meant.
For gratitude rewires the brain, creating a new way,
A path of joy and peace, where hearts will stay.

When we say "thank you," we send out a wave,
A ripple of gratitude, for the blessings we crave.
And in return, the Universe responds in kind,
With abundance and joy, peace of mind.

Gratitude is the light that guides us through,
In moments of darkness, it brings a new view.
For every challenge, every trial we face,
Gratitude helps us find our place.

Cultivate gratitude, let it grow,
In our hearts and minds, let it flow.
For in gratitude's embrace, we find our power,
To create a life that's rich and flower.

Impact of a Beautiful Soul

In the sea of thoughts, where beauty is born,
It's not just the face, but the mind that's adorned.
For beauty transcends the physical form,
It's the soul's reflection, in the eye of the storm.

Beauty is the kindness, that shines from within,
It's the empathy, the compassion, the love that
we spin.
It's the way we see the world, with wonder and
grace,
It's the joy that we share, in every embrace.

True beauty lies in the way we connect,
In the stories we tell, the words we select.
It's in the way we appreciate art,
And find beauty in every beating heart.

It's in the way we forgive, and the way we heal,
In the way we show gratitude, and the love we
reveal.
It's in the strength we find, in times of despair,
And the way we rise, from moments unfair.

And when our time on earth comes to an end,
Our beautiful souls will still transcend.
Remembered in stories, in hearts so true,
A legacy of beauty, in all that we do.

So let us not be defined by our looks,
But by the way we read life's complex books.
Let us be beautiful in thoughts and in deeds,
For true beauty is found in the heart that leads.

Faith and Surrender

Trust the Universe, in its infinite grace,
For it guides us with a gentle embrace.
Even when the path seems unclear,
Know that the Universe is always near.

In every twist and turn of fate,
Trust that the Universe will navigate.
For what may seem like a detour,
Could be the Universe's way to ensure.

Trust the Universe when all seems lost,
For it may be redirecting at no cost.
In the chaos and the unknown,

Trust that you are not alone.

Trust the Universe, in its silent grace,
Does it hear our prayers, in this vast space?
In the chaos of life, where do we find peace,
Is it in surrender, or in our own release?

I know trusting is hard when life is askew,
But surrendering brings a different view.
So let go of the worry, let go of the fear,
Trust the Universe, for it's always here.

In every moment, in every way,
Trust the Universe, come what may.

Colors of the Soul

In a world that's often gray and dull,
Some souls stand out, vibrant and full.
They've faced their demons, endured the storm,
Yet in life's small wonders, they find a form.

The most beautiful, they see life's hues,
In every moment, they refuse to lose.
Through hardship and pain, they still find glee,
In life's simple joys, they dance free.

In a world that can be harsh and cold,
They plant seeds of kindness, a story untold.
With hearts so pure, and spirits so light,
They shine like stars in the darkest of night.

Through valleys of sorrow, they walk with
grace,
Finding beauty in every place.
In the laughter of children, in the song of the
birds,
In the whispered breeze, their joy is heard.

Their past a guide, not a weight,
They embrace life, no room for hate.
Admired for their spirits, admired for their
smiles,
They make the world brighter, mile after mile.

For in every trial, they find a way,
To see the beauty, come what may.
The most beautiful souls, in colors they dwell,
Their story of resilience, they beautifully tell.

They teach us to cherish, to love, and to give,
To embrace every moment, to truly live.
In their eyes, we see a world so true,
A world painted in every color, a world anew.

So let us learn from these beautiful souls,
To see the world in its entirety, in its whole.
For in their light, we find our own,
In their colors, our hearts are sewn.

Imperfectly Perfect

In a garden of roses, so perfect and neat,
There bloomed a flower, with petals unique.
Its stem was crooked, its petals askew,
But to the gardener's eye, it was a view.

For beauty lies in the eyes of the beholder,
Imperfectly perfect, like a boulder.
In the garden, this flower stood out,
Its imperfections, what it's all about.

The other flowers whispered, they couldn't see,
Why this flower was chosen, why it was free.
But the gardener smiled, with eyes so bright,
"Beauty," he said, "is not just in sight.

It's in the story, the journey, the tale,
In every imperfection, there's a sail.
In a world where beauty is not just skin deep,
But in the heart, the soul, where it leaps."

And so, this flower, imperfectly perfect,
Became a symbol, a heartfelt connect.
For in its imperfections, it showed,
That beauty is not just what's bestowed.

It's in the flaws, the scars, the marks,
In every imperfection, it sparks.
So let us be like this flower, so rare,
Embracing our imperfections, without a care.

For beauty lies in the eyes of the beholder,
Imperfectly perfect, like a boulder.
In every flaw, in every part,
We find beauty that's in our heart.

Sea Whispers

On the shores of Goa, where the sea meets the
sky,
I stood in awe, as time floated by.
The tranquil water whispered secrets untold,
A vast expanse of blue, a sight to behold.
I gazed at the sky, so vast and wide,
A canvas of dreams, where stars reside.
The universe, with its infinite grace,
Offered me solace, in this peaceful place.
Around me, people played and laughed,
In their joyous moments, the world seemed half,
But in the quiet of my thoughts, I found,
A deeper connection, to life's profound journey.
As I walked along the shore,
Picking up shells, washed up by the ocean's roar,
Each shell a story, a memory from the past,
Reminding me that time moves fast.

The sea, the sky, the shells beneath my feet,
A reminder that life is bittersweet.
But in this moment, I find peace,
A connection to the past, a sense of release.
The universe has much to offer, I realize,
If only we pause, and open our eyes.
To connect the dots, to see the signs,
To expand our thinking, beyond the confines.
So I'll treasure these moments, by the sea,
Where time stands still, and I am free.
For in the beauty of the shore,
I find myself, and so much more.

Mystical Moon

In the velvety expanse of the night,
The moon hangs like a shimmering light,
With its craters and spots, it's not flawless, they
say,
Yet its beauty enchants, in its own mysterious
way.
'Chand bhi daag hai,' the saying goes,
But in its waxing and waning, a story it shows,
Of growth and of change, of cycles and phases,
Like the moon, we too, in life's endless mazes.
In its waxing, a promise of new beginnings,
A time for setting goals, for dreaming and
winning,
As it reaches its fullness, so do our dreams,
A radiant glow, or so it seems.
But as it begins to wane, a lesson it teaches,

Of letting go, of releasing what no longer
reaches,
For in the darkness, a new cycle begins,
A chance for rebirth, for growth, for our sins.
Moon rituals, a manifestation of this eternal
dance,
A reminder of life's ever-changing stance,
From setting intentions to letting go,
In the moon's phases, a deeper truth to know.
In its silvery light, I find peace, a sense of calm,
a sweet release,
The moon, in all its celestial might,
Fills my heart with wonder, pure and bright.
Under its glow, worries cease, in its embrace, all
troubles decrease.

Let us embrace our flaws, like the moon's spots,
For in our imperfections, our beauty plots,
And like the moon, let us wax and wane,
Growing, evolving, in life's cosmic terrain.

www.ingramcontent.com/pod-product-compliance
Lightning Source LLC
La Vergne TN
LVHW021245200726
843509LV00012B/1596